Dramatis Personae

Author / Sir Ruthven Glenaloon / Bus Conductor. . . Baritone
Gripper / The Spirit of Romance. . . Bass
Herbert. . . Tenor
Lady Rockalda. . . Mezzo or Contralto
Alice Grey. . . Soprano

A Sensation Novel

A Sensation Novel

W.S. Gilbert

MINT EDITIONS

A Sensation Novel was first published in 1871.

This edition published by Mint Editions 2021.

ISBN 9781513296876 | E-ISBN 9781513298375

Published by Mint Editions®

MINT
EDITIONS

minteditionbooks.com

Publishing Director: Jennifer Newens
Design & Production: Rachel Lopez Metzger
Project Manager: Micaela Clark
Typesetting: Westchester Publishing Services

Volume 1

<u>No. 1: Music for Curtain.</u> *The* Author *discovered seated at a table writing. He has finished his first volume, and is at a loss how to begin the second.*

Author: I do not know how it is, but I cannot get on with this novel. I've been nearly a week at work, and I have only just finished the first volume. A week! Why, I ought to have finished three volumes in a week! Am I not assisted by supernatural agency? Have I not entered into a compact with the Demon of Romance, by which I am able to turn out fifty, three-volumed novels per annum? And, on the strength of that compact, haven't I entered into an agreement with my publishers to supply them, under a heavy forfeiture, with that number of sensation novels every year until further notice? To be sure I have. But here I am in a fix. Well, shall I hesitate to summon my ghostly adviser to my aid? Certainly not! Now for the incantation that will bring him to my side.

(*He takes a huge saucepan and places the following ingredients into it during the Incantation*)

<u>No. 2: Incantation.</u>

(*Spoken through music*)
    Take of best quill pens a score,
    Take of ink a pint or more,
    Take of foolscap half a ream,
    Take, oh take, a convict's dream,
    Lynch pin, fallen from a carriage,
    Forged certificate of marriage,
    Money wrongly won at whist,
    Finger of a bigamist,
    Cobweb from mysterious vaults,
    Arsenic sold as Epsom Salts,
    Pocket-knife with blood-stained blade,
    Telegram, some weeks delayed,
    Parliamentary committee,
    Joint stock panic in the city,
    Trial at Old Bailey bar,

Take a Newgate Calendar,
Take a common jury's finding,
Take a most attractive binding,
Hold the saucepan by the handle,
Boil it on a penny candle.

(*The* SPIRIT OF ROMANCE *appears.* AUTHOR *falls on his knees, terrified*)

SPIRIT: I am here!

AUTHOR: You are!

SPIRIT: What do you want with me?

AUTHOR: Help, I have just finished the first volume of my novel—and I don't know how to begin the second. By our compact, I had leave to summon you whenever I found myself in a difficulty, and you promised to help me out of it.

SPIRIT: Have you employed the characters I have lent you?—the virtuous governess, the unemployed young Sunday School teacher, the sensation detective, the wicked baronet, the beautiful fiend with the yellow hair and the panther-like movement?

AUTHOR: I have!

SPIRIT: You have made the virtuous governess in love with the Sunday School teacher? You have made her persecuted by the wicked baronet?

AUTHOR: Yes!

SPIRIT: The yellow-haired fiend with the panther-like movement is his accomplice?

AUTHOR: She is!

SPIRIT: Have you made *her* fall in love with the Sunday School teacher?

AUTHOR: Head and ears.

SPIRIT: And he treats her with disdain?

AUTHOR: He does!

SPIRIT: Humph! Have you obeyed my advice as to diet and eaten nothing but pork chops and cold plum pudding?

AUTHOR: Nothing! Look at me.

SPIRIT: You have slept with your head lower than your body?

AUTHOR: Every night.

SPIRIT: You have put live shrimps down your back to make your flesh creep?

AUTHOR: Pints of them! There are some there now (*wriggles*)

SPIRIT: You have read the "Illustrated Police News"?

AUTHOR: Through and through.

SPIRIT: You are in my power! These creatures whom I have lent you are slaves to my will. Refuse to obey me, and I withdraw them altogether. They are accepted types, and you can't get on without them.

AUTHOR: True! But tell me, what is the nature of the power you exercise over them.

SPIRIT: It is very peculiar. They are all creatures who, in their mortal condition, have been guilty of positive or negative crime, and they are compelled to personate, under my direction, those stock characters of the sensation novelist which are most opposed to their individual tastes and inclinations.

AUTHOR: Then they have an existence apart from that with which they are endowed in the novel?

SPIRIT: They have! Apart from it, but eventually subject to it; that is to say, they have wishes, schemes and plans of their own, but the fulfilment of these wishes is, for the time being, in the hands of the Author, to whom they are entrusted. They have the power of coming to life at the end of the first and second volumes, and immediately before the last chapter of the third, to talk over the events that have taken place, and to arrange plans for the future—plans which are too often frustrated by the Author's arbitrary will. This is not generally known.

AUTHOR: Do I understand you to say that at the end of the first volume they come to life?

SPIRIT: They do!

AUTHOR: I have just finished the first volume.

SPIRIT: It is now five minutes to twelve—at twelve they will be here!

AUTHOR (*going*): I've an appointment in the City which I had entirely overlooked.

SPIRIT: Won't you stay and see them?

AUTHOR: Thanks, no. One supernatural being is as much as I feel equal to at a time. I'd rather go.

No. 3a: DUET—SPIRIT and AUTHOR.

SPIRIT: In half a minute they'll be here!

AUTHOR: I shake and quake with sense of fear!

SPIRIT: The Baronet—the maiden fair,
    The Panther with the yellow hair;
AUTHOR: The Tutor, too, with fate ill-starred,
    Detective, too, from Scotland Yard,
BOTH: All will be here!
SPIRIT: They'll be plotting—they'll be planning—
    With the cunning of a Canning,
AUTHOR: All my plans they'll be upsetting,
    Novel schemes they'll be begetting,
SPIRIT: Both the baronet and the maiden,
    And the tutor, sorrow-laden,
AUTHOR: And the panther with invective,
    'Gainst the Scotland Yard Detective,
BOTH: All will be here!
AUTHOR: And this is so?
SPIRIT: Yes! to the letter.
AUTHOR: I think I'll go!
SPIRIT: I think you'd better!
BOTH: They will be here.
(*Exeunt*)

No. 3b: Melodrame.

(*Enter Lady Rockalda*)
ROCKALDA: So the first volume's at an end, and once more we, the
    puppets of a sensation author's will, are launched upon our
    eventful careers. In the course of the ten years during which
    I have been compelled to obey my prolific author's will, I, the
    beautiful yellow-haired fiend of sensational fiction, have worked
    my wicked way through no less than seventy-five sensation
    novels! I shudder when I think of the amount of evil I have done.
    I shudder still more, when I think of the amount of evil I have
    still to do! But I must not repine for I have deserved it all. When
    I was a mortal I was the indulgent mother of five unruly boys, an
    easy-going peace-loving mother. I allowed them to have their own
    way, and as a punishment for my culpable neglect I am compelled
    to serve my Author's will, during the term of his natural life! It's a
    hard fate, but I have deserved it, and I must not repine.

Like a motherly old lady,
With demure old-fashioned ways,
In a cottage snug and shady,
I should like to spend my days.
Through the village I could toddle,
To relieve the old and lame;
I would be the very model
Of a motherly old dame.

But my tastes and inclinations
Must be hidden out of sight;
Oh! Forgive my lamentations,
I am miserable quite.
For propriety's affliction
Guilty deeds I must prepare;
I'm the lovely fiend of fiction,
With the yellow, yellow hair.

With voice and gait mysterious,
Expression fixed and serious,
And manner most imperious,
I work my charge.
In love unbridled, as in hate,
I wheedle, coax and fascinate,
Then murder, rob, assassinate
Mankind at large.

Like a motherly old lady,
With demure, old-fashioned ways,
In a cottage snug and shady,
I should like to end my days.
But for innocents' affliction
Guilty deeds I must prepare;
I'm the lovely fiend of fiction,
With the yellow, yellow hair.

No. 5: Melodrame.

(*Enter* Sir Ruthven Glenaloon, *dressed as an Officer of Footguards*)

Ruthven: Rockalda, this is a melancholy meeting.

Rockalda: It is, but we have deserved it all.

Ruthven: We have, but it is very hard to be a wicked baronet against one's will. Why, I was the softest hearted fellow alive—when I *was* alive.

Rockalda: But soft hearted as you were, you did a deal of mischief in your time.

Ruthven: I did! Let me confess my misdeeds: I never saw a beggar in the streets but I gave him a penny—shocking, wasn't it?

Rockalda: Terrible, indeed! But you did worse than that—you—you encouraged organ grinders.

Ruthven: I did, I did! but spare me your reproaches, for now I see the enormity of my misconduct, and I am undergoing a bitter expiation.

Rockalda: Yes, you are the wicked baronet of sensational fiction, and it serves you right.

Ruthven: But where are we?

Rockalda: This is a ruined summer house, overlooking the Thames. The river runs under the window and beneath the floor, which is full of traps—which open with springs, and many murders have been committed in this very room.

Ruthven: But why does the Author live here?

Rockalda: This room stimulates his imagination. The first volume treats of dark mysterious deeds, done in the vilest haunts of the most abandoned ruffians he could find.

Ruthven: Then the abandoned ruffian has abandoned it for the present?

Rockalda: He has! Have no fear.

Ruthven: I don't like this. I'm a timid, nervous man, and I don't feel at all comfortable in the place.

Rockalda: Take comfort. The second volume will treat of high life. For that, he has secured part of Windsor Castle. The third will take place in Africa, and we shall then find ourselves in Barbary. It is his way, and we are all the slaves of his fancy.

Ruthven: But where's the good young man of the novel? He ought to be here!

No. 6a: Melodrame.

(*Enter* HERBERT, *dressed in semi-clerical fashion, with a very sanctified appearance*)

HERBERT: He is here! my Rockalda!

ROCKALDA: My Herbert! (*They embrace*)

HERBERT: At last we meet. Let me see, the last time we met was at the end of the Indian novel—"Black as a boot is he!"

ROCKALDA: It was. You were then a mild young artist travelling in India.

HERBERT: I was; and you were the yellow-haired Begum of the Rajah of Babbetyboobledore.

RUTHVEN: And I—ha! ha! I was Nana Sahib! It's some comfort to reflect that I am to go through this novel with a clean face.

HERBERT: But with very dirty hands.

RUTHVEN: Yes, that's my invariable fate. Oh, I say, ain't I a bad character!

ROCKALDA: Shocking!

RUTHVEN: We've only got to the end of the first volume, and I've already committed a burglary, a forgery, a falsification of a baptismal entry, and I'll lay twenty to one I try to murder you, Herbert, before I'm done.

HERBERT: I'll lay you twenty to one you don't succeed.

RUTHVEN: No, you're the good young man, and it wouldn't do— you've got to marry Alice.

HERBERT: Bah! Don't remind me of that.

RUTHVEN: My Alice, whom I love so devotedly, and who loves me.

ROCKALDA: Yes, *out* of the novel.

RUTHVEN: Exactly! *In* the novel she detests me. Fortunately, we have an opportunity at the end of each volume of shaking off the detestable attributes with which the Author invests us, and of appearing for an hour or so in our own true light. In my true light Alice worships me.

HERBERT: Well, we've deserved it all.

RUTHVEN: We have, we have. What did you do on Earth?

HERBERT: I! Listen. I frequented music halls and sang comic songs, and as a punishment I have to represent the Author's good young man during the term of his natural life. Horrible, isn't it?

ALL: Most horrible!

ROCKALDA: Well, I don't complain, only it was too bad to make a girl of twenty of me.

HERBERT: A girl of twenty! You're a girl of a thousand.

ROCKALDA: My love!

RUTHVEN: Yes, you look more than twenty.

ROCKALDA: More than twenty? Why, I'm five and forty if I'm a day.

RUTHVEN: No, forty—I should say.

ROCKALDA: Forty-five—upon my honour.

HERBERT: You will always be young in *my* eyes.

ROCKALDA: Under these circumstances I shall be content to live in them for ever.

RUTHVEN: But the necessities of the story require that you shall pass yourself off for twenty. You know that you, the grown-up daughter of Tom Sittybank, the bus conductor, passed yourself off as the daughter of the Duke of Ben-Nevis, Lady Rockalda, whom you brought up as Alice Grey, the foundling, so you *must* pass yourself off as a being no older than the so-called Alice Grey, whose title and position in society you have assumed.

ROCKALDA: And then to make me fall hopelessly in love with Herbert, hopelessly! He spurns me—loads me with reproaches, and tells me he is familiar with the details of my disgraceful career!

HERBERT: But I only spurn you *in* the novel—*out* of the novel I worship the very ground you walk on. It is an agreeable relief after making love for a whole volume to that ridiculously insipid creature, Alice Grey—I say it is a relief to find yourself in the society, though for a few moments, of so superior and well-matured a person as my Rockalda. (*They embrace*)

No. 6b: Melodrame.

(*Enter* ALICE GREY, *a very demure modest-looking governess*)

ALICE: Ha! Ha! My devoted Herbert in the arms of the detestable Lady Rockalda! What would the Author say?

No. 7: QUARTET—LADY ROCKALDA, ALICE, SIR RUTHVEN and HERBERT.

ALICE: Goodness gracious!
　　How audacious!

　　　　　　　　　　　　　　　W.S. GILBERT

What deception you disclose!
My adorer,
On the floor-er,
At the base Rockalda's toes!

HERBERT, ROCKALDA, SIR RUTHVEN: Ah, confusion!
This delusion!
Will destroy her, goodness knows!
It's affecting
Her detecting,
Me/You preparing to propose.

ALICE: I will go and bring my action,
I will bring it, I declare!
Oh, despair! Oh, distraction!
Oh, distraction! Oh, despair.

HERBERT, ROCKALDA, SIR RUTHVEN: She will go and bring her action,
She will bring it, she declare!
Oh, despair! Oh, distraction!
Oh, distraction! Oh, despair.

HERBERT: Now look here! Alice, I've been spooneying after you, writing poetry to you, and kissing your *carte de visite* through the entire length of a whole volume, and tomorrow morning I shall have to begin again. Do, for goodness sake, let me enjoy myself during the few minutes of relaxation that are permitted me between the volumes.

ALICE: My good soul, don't suppose for one moment that I intend to interrupt you. Let us make the most of these happy intervals, for I'm sure you will marry me at the end of the third volume.

HERBERT: Horrible prospect!

ALICE: Horrible indeed!

RUTHVEN: But Alice, you may not marry him after all. He may prove unworthy of you.

HERBERT: That's not likely. I'm dreadfully good—I feel it!

ALICE: Oh! Ruthven, my love, when the Author set you on to persecute me with your attention and contrive all sorts of plans to carry me off and marry me against my will, he little dreamt how ardently I hoped that your nefarious schemes would be successful. But, no, that irritating Curate whom I love so desperately *in* the novel, and detest so heartily *out* of it, always interferes to balk your plans.

HERBERT: Yes, I am a donkey *in* the novel.

ALICE: A donkey? You're a bashful noodle!

HERBERT: I was rather bold in the scene with you in the pine forest—don't you remember? Where's the Ms.? Oh, here it is—(*Reads*) "Miss Alice, said Herbert—"

ALICE: *Miss* Alice! In a pine forest—by moonlight, too. *Miss* Alice, oh, you great donkey!

HERBERT: Oh, but I warmed up afterwards. (*Reads*) "Miss Alice, I fear your stoney-hearted guardian will never relent."

RUTHVEN: That's me; I'm the stoney-hearted guardian.

HERBERT: (*Reads*) "You are very formal, Herbert, replied Alice."

ALICE: Yes, I should think so, Sir Ruthven would have known better—Wouldn't you, dear?

HERBERT: But you were so confoundedly proper. Besides, I was only putting out a feeler. (*Reads*) "Miss Grey—Alice, dear Alice, dearest Alice, I *may* call you dearest—Alice may I not?" That was warm.

ALICE: Not a bit too warm after the demure encouragement I gave you—go on!

HERBERT: (*Reads*) "I may call you dearest, Alice, may I not?" "I cannot help what you choose to call me, said the pretty girl." Pretty girl, I like that.

ALICE: So do I!

HERBERT: (*Reads*) "They were alone—with the moon. They heard the throbbings of each other's hearts, which beat like rival watches, wound up in each other! He drew her gently towards him, and imprinted a solitary kiss on her soft—"

ALICE: (*Taking the* Ms. *from him*) "On her soft little hand!" Oh you goose!

ALL: Ha! Ha! Ha!

ALICE: But that's nothing to what followed, listen! (*Reads*) "She turned away, Oh, Herbert, said she, bashfully raising her purple eyes to the spot where he had been sitting—but he was gone." There! Left me alone in the pine forest at midnight.

HERBERT: But I heard footsteps and ran, that you might not be compromised. It was very considerate.

RUTHVEN: The footsteps were mine.

ALICE: (*Fondly*) They were.

RUTHVEN: I behaved better than he did in the scene that followed, didn't I?

ALICE: You did. It was rapture.

RUTHVEN: (*Taking the* Ms.) "Alice, said the Baronet, his cold, evil grey eye lighting with a horrible fire. At last you are in my power! I heard you were in the forest, and I determined to find you. Alice covered her eyes with her hands. She tried to scream, but terror had rendered her speechless."

ALICE: Yes, it was delightful. I remember it all. Let's go through it again.

RUTHVEN: You were alone with that penniless curate.

ALICE: I was.

RUTHVEN: You love him.

ALICE: I do. Why should I blush to own it? But how know you this?

RUTHVEN: I lay concealed beneath yon blackberry bush, and I overheard all.

ALICE: Then it was unmanly done.

RUTHVEN: Not so, pretty one, for I also love you, and in love, as in war, all schemes are fair. (*Taking her round the waist*)

ALICE: Unhand me, monster!

RUTHVEN: Not so, pretty one. Listen! A coach and six is in readiness in the thickest part of the forest, and I have minions who will drive you where I will. Salisbury Plain is barely fifty leagues away, a clergyman in full canonicals, and an aged pew-opener are awaiting us at Stonehenge, and he will speak the words that will make you mine.

ALICE: Unhand me, coward, or my shrieks shall bring those around you who will make you repent the day you laid a hand on old John Grey's daughter, help! help! help!

HERBERT: (*Rushing forward and seizing* SIR RUTHVEN) Monster! unhand that lady!

ALICE: There! (*Aside*) You were always interfering when you were not wanted, just as we were getting on so comfortably together.

HERBERT: Well it's the Author's fault—(*resuming*) Monster! unhand that lady! Alice, has he dared to offer violence?

ALICE: He has!

HERBERT: Ha! Then let this deadly blow avenge the dastard outrage (*prepares to strike*)

RUTHVEN: Ah! never mind the deadly blow.

HERBERT: I delivered it right from the shoulder between the eyes.

RUTHVEN: You did, I remember it perfectly.

HERBERT: I hope I didn't hurt you much?

RUTHVEN: Ah, well, never mind, it's a painful subject; at all events I got over it, but wasn't it a delicious scene?

ALICE: Heavenly. Oh! Ruthven, if that donkey hadn't interrupted us we should have been comfortably married at Stonehenge and all would have ended happily.

HERBERT: I'm sure I wish it had.

ROCKALDA: So indeed do I. *We* might have been happy. Do you remember the chapter in which I first fell in love with you?

HERBERT: Perfectly! It was at the old limekiln.

ROCKALDA: It was. Sir Ruthven set me on to lure you to the limekiln, with my panther-like movement and the lurid fascination of my yellow hair.

RUTHVEN: I did! "Rockalda," said I, "engage him in conversation at the brink of the limekiln. I will come upon him from behind, and, having stunned him with one unerring blow, I will consume his body in the lime, and not so much as a button shall be left to tell the tale."

ROCKALDA: Yes, but I wouldn't agree to that. "No, Sir Ruthven," I said; "if there is murder to be done, I will do it alone." I lured you to the limekiln under a promise that when I had got you there I would reveal the secret of your birth.

HERBERT: You did! I came! "Madam," said I, "I am here at your request. You have a secret that concerns me intimately."

ROCKALDA: I have!

HERBERT: Why turn your face away from me?

ROCKALDA: No matter—it is my whim. (*Aside*) I dare not look upon him, or he will read my deadly purpose in my eyes.

HERBERT: You tell me that you possess the secret of my birth? Oh, madam, reveal it!

ROCKALDA: Listen, and I will reveal all! I have brought you here to murder you. Tremble, for your last hour has come. (*She turns and seizes him by the throat. A ray of moonlight falls on his face*) Merciful heavens! how lovely!

HERBERT: I did not expect this. Strike, woman! if you have the heart to do so.

ROCKALDA: Heart! I never had a heart till now. (*Aside*) It is the face of an angel.

HERBERT: Unfortunately I am a Sunday School teacher or I would resist.

ROCKALDA: Resistance were useless. Feel that arm!

HERBERT: The muscles are of steel.

ROCKALDA: Exactly; listen! I am here to kill you, but I have seen your face and I love you. Marry me and your life is spared; refuse and I toss your body into the middle of yonder limekiln, and every trace of you will be consumed.

HERBERT: Marry you! Never! Strike if my hour is come. (*She raises dagger*) Now, we can't get on without Gripper, the detective.

ROCKALDA: Ah! where *is* Gripper? He ought to have been here before this.

ALL: Gripper! Gripper! Gripper!

No. 8: Melodrame.

(*Enter* GRIPPER *dressed as a Grand Turk*)

GRIPPER: Here I am! How de do?

ROCKALDA: You're late, Gripper!

GRIPPER: Well, I'm afraid I am; but then I am a sensation detective, and sensation detectives always *are* late. The reason's obvious enough. If the detective of a sensation novel were not always just too late, the novel would come to an end long before its time. If I bring to justice all the villains of the novel in the course of the first volume, what's to prevent the virtuous governess marrying the good young curate at once, and if she does that there's an end of everything.

ALICE: Of course! Why if Gripper hadn't been just too late throughout the first volume all would have ended happily at once; I should have married the man of my choice and been miserable for life fifty pages ago.

HERBERT: My dear Gripper, we ought to be very much obliged to you. The longer you can delay that catastrophe the better pleased we shall all be. But why are you dressed like that?

GRIPPER: It is a disguise, that I may follow you about without attracting too much attention.

ALL: Ridiculous! Preposterous!

ROCKALDA: I don't complain, I don't care what happens so that I am not separated from the good young curate.

HERBERT: And I don't care what happens so that I am not removed from my yellow-haired panther.

ALICE: And I don't care so that I continue to be persecuted by the infamous Sir Ruthven.

RUTHVEN: And I don't care so that I am allowed sometimes to see the spotless innocent Alice.

GRIPPER: Very well! then don't complain of my being always too late. If I am only once in time—*only once*—there's an end of everything, and the governess marries the curate on the spot.

ALICE: Horrible!

HERBERT: Horrible indeed!

ALICE: (*To Herbert*) I hate you more than ever!

HERBERT: Believe me, your sentiments are sincerely reciprocated.

ALICE: (*To Ruthven*) But there is still hope, dear Ruthven; after all the Author may intend us for each other. The virtuous young woman has so often been married to the good young man that the public must begin to tire of the incessant repetition.

RUTHVEN: Yes, but you see I'm such an awful villain!

ALICE: So you are! But couldn't I convert you?

RUTHVEN: *You* could—if anyone could. But I'm afraid I'm too far gone for that—No, you'll have to marry the Curate, and live happily ever after.

HERBERT: Marry and live happily ever after! And this is a novel that pretends to give a picture of life as it is. Yes, I'm afraid, Alice, we are booked for one another.

ROCKALDA: But how much better it would be—how much more original if Alice were to reform Ruthven, and you were to reform me. You two good people would be of some use then.

HERBERT: Ah, I'm afraid there's no chance of reforming *you*, my love—You don't feel it coming on, do you?

ROCKALDA: Not a bit—I'm worse than ever.

GRIPPER: Still there are two volumes to come, and who knows what may happen.

ROCKALDA: Yes, but if we are to be reformed, what's the use of you?

GRIPPER: Just what I want to know! One thing is quite certain. As long as I go on, assuming these preposterous disguises I shall never contrive to bring you or anybody else to justice. Why, I am as conspicuous as the Crystal Palace fireworks.

(*Clock strikes one*)

W.S. GILBERT

Rockalda: One o'clock! Our time is up, and we must retire into our sensation characters. Good-bye, Herbert, we shall meet again at the end of the second volume. Ah, who knows what may happen in the interval.

Herbert: Whatever happens *in* the novel nothing can alter my sentiments towards you, *out* of it.

Ruthven: Alice, farewell, Alice, my own, my loved one.

Alice: Farewell, Ruthven; we shall meet at the end of the second volume. In the meantime, persecute me, Ruthven, as much as you please. You can't think how much I like it.

No. 9: Finale To Volume 1—Ensemble.

Alice: Increase my woes,
    My best of foes;
    Oh, follow me, worry me, harry me,
    And if you can,
    Cut out that man,
    And marry me, marry me, marry me!
Sir Ruthven: With dark design,
    To make you mine;
    I'll follow you, worry you, trouble you!
    So single stay,
    If I've may way,
    I'll double you, double you, double you!
Herbert: Oh, panther fair,
    With yellow hair,
    And beauty almost magical,
    If we should part,
    'Twould break my heart;
    Ah, tragical, tragical, tragical!
Rockalda: Oh! you who rule
    A Sunday School
    Of babes in their minority,
    Though forty-four,
    I bow to your
    Authority—thority, thority!
Gripper: Go on, my friends,
    Pursue your ends;

I'll keep an open eye to you!
Alas, if I'm
But once in time,
Good-bye to you, bye to you, bye to you!

END OF VOLUME 1

Volume 2

No. 10a: Introduction.

No. 10b: Melodrame.

(*Enter* LADY ROCKALDA)

ROCKALDA: Well, here we are at the end of the second volume, and a nice time I've had of it.

(*Enter* SIR RUTHVEN, *languidly*)

RUTHVEN: Eh! What's the matter?

ROCKALDA: Matter? Matter enough. Why, as you know, Herbert was sent off at the beginning of the second volume as a missionary to Central Africa and he hasn't returned yet.

RUTHVEN: Poor Rockalda.

ROCKALDA: I wonder how much longer I'm to be kept without him.

RUTHVEN: Well, but he's not much good to you, you know. He despises your love and avoids you whenever he can.

ROCKALDA: I know he does *in* the novel, but still it is something to be with him and to see him sometimes, and we had to do without him for a whole volume. Ah, here he is! My Herbert!

HERBERT: My Rockalda! At last we meet!

ROCKALDA: Tell me when—oh, when do you return from Central Africa?

HERBERT: Alas! Not for several chapters.

ROCKALDA: This is indeed hard. I don't like this novel at all.

HERBERT: It's shameful! The publisher told the Author that I was getting so confoundedly insipid that no reader would stand me, and he must get rid of me somehow, so he sent me to Central Africa for seven years. I'm there now, and I am very much afraid I shall not return till the last chapter. Transportation for seven years is rather too serious a punishment. Is Alice all right?

RUTHVEN: Yes, and more lovely than ever.

HERBERT: Oh! I'm sorry for that. You haven't carried her off and married her?

RUTHVEN: No, not yet.

HERBERT: What a fellow you are! I've been out of your way all the volume. You might have done that for me.

RUTHVEN: I'd have done it for myself with pleasure, but I'm not a free agent. I did try.

ROCKALDA: That he did, and I helped him.

HERBERT: Bless you! Tell me all about it.

RUTHVEN: What! don't you know?

HERBERT: How should I? I've been out of the volume altogether.

RUTHVEN: True! Alice, as you are aware, was to have gone to Africa with you.

HERBERT: Yes! she was to have joined me at Liverpool, but by some fortunate chance I was spared that infliction—she never turned up and I sailed without her.

RUTHVEN: Exactly—I managed that—You see that both Rockalda and I were interested in preventing that. I, because I loved Alice. Rockalda, because she loved you. She was to travel by the nine o'clock express to Liverpool from London, so what do you think I did?

HERBERT: Sent her a Bradshaw perhaps to confuse her and make her miss her train.

RUTHVEN: No, better than that. I slew the pointsman at Rugby Junction and turned the train on to the Midland line.

HERBERT: How good of you, well, what followed?

RUTHVEN: I don't know, for just as I had accomplished my object a Red Indian struck me on the head with his tomahawk and I fell senseless to the ground.

ROCKALDA: I can tell you what followed—I was in the train—After the train had been turned on to the Midland line I crept cautiously along the carriages as we entered the tunnel, strangled the engine driver, dressed myself in his clothes, and drove the train safely to Leeds.

HERBERT: You changed in the tunnel? (*Horrified*)

ROCKALDA: Yes, it was quite dark.

HERBERT: Very thoughtful of the Author. My dear Rockalda, I owe you an unspeakable debt of gratitude. But what followed?

ROCKALDA: A fearful discovery. On arriving at Leeds, as the girl's ticket was for Liverpool, she was brought face to face with the station-master, who turned out to be—start not—her father, the Duke of Ben-Nevis, who for purposes of his own, had quitted his own lofty station for a *station* of a totally different description.

HERBERT: And he recognised her?

ROCKALDA: He did.

HERBERT: But how? for he had always accepted you as his daughter.

ROCKALDA: By a singular family feature, hereditary in every direct female member of the Ben-Nevis line, the back hair of all the daughters of the Dukes of Ben-Nevis has always grown in the form of a ducal coronet. He recognised her at once, and discovered that I, who had all along passed as his daughter, was an imposter.

HERBERT: Strange! But I noticed the same ducal peculiarity in your own back hair.

ROCKALDA: Yes, that puzzled his Grace at first. "How is this?" said he, "I have but one daughter, and yet here are two daughters whose back hair grows naturally in the form hereditary in our family. Which of them is mine?" And he wept bitterly.

HERBERT: Poor old gentleman; and how was the matter decided?

ROCKALDA: "Stay," said he, "a thought"; and so saying he clutched at Alice's back hair, which strongly resisted his efforts. He then clutched at mine. Alas! it came off in his hand.

HERBERT: Merciful powers! then that mass of yellow hair is—

ROCKALDA: A considerable portion of it, false!

HERBERT: You never told me this.

ROCKALDA: Attribute my reticence to maidenly reserve; it were unmaidenly for a girl to refer to any details of her toilet in the presence of a Sunday School teacher.

HERBERT: Quite out of the question. But what became of Alice?

ROCKALDA: She fled, alarmed at the Duke's extraordinary behaviour, and she has never been heard of since.

HERBERT: Then she does not know she is his daughter?

ROCKALDA: Not yet.

RUTHVEN: (*Madly*) Ha! Ha! Ha!

HERBERT: What is the matter with *you*? Is your back hair false too?

RUTHVEN: No, no; but still I am desperately unhappy.

HERBERT: Because you haven't yet persuaded Alice to marry you?

RUTHVEN: No, not that! I can't expect to bring that about; she loathes me *in* the novel, but I did think we would have been happy *out* of it.

ROCKALDA: Well, can't you?

RUTHVEN: I'm afraid not. I'm afraid that Alice is not the Duke's daughter after all. A fearful presentiment suggests to me that Alice, the lovely, the divine Alice, whom I worship with a devotion absolutely unparalleled, is—ha! ha!—my grand-daughter!

HERBERT: Then you would be—

RUTHVEN: Her grandfather! I've just recollected that in the first chapter of the novel your sister—that is to say, my second daughter—had a daughter of her own, a baby whom she deserted when only three days old. She left her on a doorstep in Belgrave Square, and I am ashamed to say she did it at my suggestion.

HERBERT: You're a bad lot!

RUTHVEN: Ain't I? Desperate! However, there was one redeeming point in her conduct, her choosing Belgrave Square. "Lucy," said I, "leave it on a doorstep in Seven Dials." "Never!" said she. "I love my babe better than life itself. Its happiness is everything to me, and its prosperity in life is my most anxious care. It shall be launched on its career under the most fashionable circumstances, and I should be neglecting my duty as a mother if I did leave it on any doorstep short of Belgrave Square." She left it in Belgrave Square, and the babe was adopted by a nobleman. Herbert! Rockalda! I'm very much afraid that the Lady Rockalda, who was put out to nurse with us, and whom you are personating, is that unhappy babe.

HERBERT: Terrible!

RUTHVEN: Hush! she comes! Leave us!

(*Enter* ALICE)

ALICE: Ruthven! (*They embrace*) Why turn from me so coldly? We have not met since the end of the first volume. Let us make the most of the short time during which we can be together.

RUTHVEN: Alice, had you ever a father?

ALICE: No!

RUTHVEN: Nor a mother?

ALICE: Never!

RUTHVEN: Are you sure of that?

ALICE: Quite.

RUTHVEN: Then I must have been mistaken. It has occurred to me that I might have been your grandfather; now, a woman, so I have heard, may not marry her grandfather.

ALICE: You have been rightly informed.

RUTHVEN: But as the grandfather is the father of the father, and you have never had a father for me to be father of, it is impossible that I can be the father of the father you never had. And yet, on the other hand, if you never had a father or a mother, who were your parents?

ALICE: That is a question that has haunted me night and day.

No. 11a: BALLAD—ALICE.

No father's care, that I'm aware,
Have I been cherished by;
No mother's smile did e'er beguile
My joyous infancy.
That I'm alive, and grow and thrive,
I know, indeed, full well,
But how, alas! it came to pass
I cannot, cannot tell.

A father's pinch might make me flinch,
As you're no doubt aware;
A mother's tweak upon the cheek
Is very hard to bear;
But harder yet to owe a debt
To no progenitor;
I would die content, if I
Could be accounted for.

RUTHVEN: Let me unveil a frightful tale—
A tale of fraud, a tale of crime!
ALICE: If aught you find upon your mind,
Proceed—

No. 11b: SONG—SIR RUTHVEN.

Well, once upon a time—

A nobleman dressed in a close-fitting mask,
His figure a domino mantling,
Brought a child to my cottage and gave me the task
Of rearing the poor little bantling.
Oh! you were that babe, as you shortly will see
(*My sin this the time to retrieve is*);
The mysterious noble who brought you to me,
Was the eminent Duke of Ben-Nevis!

My daughter, though twenty years older, or so,
Was extremely like you in the face, miss;
So she popped herself into the cradle, you know,
And passed herself off in your place, miss.
'Twas Rockalda, my daughter, who did it, I say
(*Which a terrible crime to achieve is*)!
And you, who have hitherto passed as Miss Grey,
Are the child of the Duke of Ben-Nevis!

(*Exit* SIR RUTHVEN)

ALICE: Upon my word, this is a pretty state of things! So it seems that I, who have had to pass through two volumes as a quiet, humble nursery governess, am a lady of rank and fortune! This must be enquired into.

No. 11c: Melodrame.

(*Enter* LADY ROCKALDA)

ALICE: So ma'am! you're an imposter! It seems that you have passed yourself off as the daughter of the Duke of Ben-Nevis, and caused me, his real daughter, to be brought up as an obscure and penniless governess.

ROCKALDA: My dear Alice, don't excite yourself. You have been recognised by the Duke as his daughter, and thoughout the next volume you will no doubt occupy your proper station. If you hadn't run away just as the discovery was made you would have been reinstated long ago.

ALICE: No doubt, but I did not know till a minute ago that it was through your agency that this shameful imposition was brought about.

ROCKALDA: Now don't be unreasonable, are we not all in the Author's hands?

ALICE: Certainly! But you might have told me of this before!

ROCKALDA: The secret was not mine. It was the Author's!

ALICE: But dear Ruthven has just revealed it.

ROCKALDA: Then it was very unprofessional of him. He was bound in honour to keep the Author's secret. It is not at all like Sir Ruthven to commit a breach of trust *out* of the novel.

ALICE: However, as you have admitted the fact, I insist on taking my rank immediately.

ROCKALDA: But, my dear girl!

ALICE: Menial! How dare you address me—*me* in such familiar terms? I am the Lady Alice.

ROCKALDA: Now don't be unreasonable.

ALICE: Begone, omnibus conductor's daughter. If you dare to address me again in such terms, this dagger, which I wear as a protection against my darling Sir Ruthven, shall teach ye better manners.

No. 12a: DUET—ALICE and ROCKALDA.

ALICE: With rage infuriate I burn!

ROCKALDA: My wishes on the point you spurn.

ALICE: Come, hand the jewels over please!

ROCKALDA: What! these—and these—and these and these?

ALICE: Yes, all; that brooch, those earrings fair,
The tiara that decks your hair!

ROCKALDA: If I refuse?

ALICE: This dagger blade,
I straightway summon to my aid.

(LADY ROCKALDA *gives jewels to* ALICE—*she puts them on*)
In rarest jewels brightly shining,
With diamonds upon my brow,
In humble garb no longer pining,
I take my true position now.

ROCKALDA: Those jewels ill befit your tatters—
Oh! dread, oh! dread the Author's rage!
For you're anticipating matters
By many and many a stirring page.

ALICE:	ROCKALDA:
Though jewels ill befit my tatters,	Those jewels ill befit your tatters—
I do not dread the Author's rage;	Oh! dread, oh! dread the Author's rage!
I like anticipating matters	For you're anticipating matters
By many and many a stirring page.	By many and many a stirring page.

No. 12b: Melodrame.

(*Enter* GRIPPER *dressed as a North American Indian*)
GRIPPER: I beg your pardon—I'm afraid I am late again.

ROCKALDA: You are! If you had been here a minute sooner, you would have been able to prevent a most outrageous robbery.

GRIPPER: Dear me! I am very sorry, but I am a detective and must act up to my character.

ROCKALDA: Surely it's part of a detective's duty to prevent the commission of crime!

GRIPPER: Oh, dear no, quite the reverse! It is a detective's duty to encourage the commission of crime, that he may detect it after it has been committed and that, just too late to bring the perpetrator to justice! Why, you might as well expect a sportsman to banish pheasants from his preserves, that he may not be put to the trouble of shooting 'em. Who has been robbing you?

ROCKALDA: Alice Grey! She compelled me at the dagger's point to hand over all my jewellery.

GRIPPER: Indeed! Place the matter in my hands, and I'll detect her with pleasure. You are certain Alice Grey committed this robbery?

ROCKALDA: Quite!

GRIPPER: (*Takes out notebook*) Then I have no hesitation in saying that suspicion points very strongly to Alice Grey.

ROCKALDA: You don't say so! Intelligent officer! Then there she is! You'd better arrest her!

GRIPPER: Arrest her! No, no, no. We don't do business like that. Arrest her! Why any fool could do that. No, I must track her down.

No. 13: SONG—GRIPPER.

When information I receive that Jones has been a-forging,
And on the proceeds of his crime is prodigally gorging,
Do you suppose I collar my friend and take him to the beak, ma'am?
Why, bless your heart, they wouldn't retain me in the force a week, ma'am.

In curious wig and quaint disguise, and strangely altered face, ma'am,
Unrecognised I follow my prey about from place to place, ma'am;
I note his hair, his eyes, his nose, his clothing and complexion,
And when I have got 'em all into my head, I set about detection.

I take his servants, one by one, and bring them all to book, ma'am,
Both man and maid of every grade, particularly his cook, ma'am;
His tradesmen then I call upon, examine 'em on their oaths, ma'am;
And the elderly man, of the Hebrew clan, who buys his left-off
    clothes, ma'am.

His father-in-law, perhaps, is buffalo hunting in the Prairies,
His aunt may keep a lodging-house in the ocean-girt Canaries;
His uncle's out in Honolulu, his neice in arctic zones, ma'am,
I find them out and talk to them before arresting Jones, ma'am.

And when my call is quite complete, and home again I fly, ma'am,
I find that Jones has gone abroad, some people are so sly, ma'am;
But I've this consolation—all the facts that I've collated,
Would surely have convicted Jones—if Jones had only waited.

(*Enter* SIR RUTHVEN)

RUTHVEN: (*Rushing at* GRIPPER) Ha! You are the North American
    that sprung upon me just as I had shunted the train, with Alice in
    it, on to the Midland line! You struck me a deadly blow.

GRIPPER: I did; I hope it didn't hurt you much! It wasn't my fault! I
    was in the Author's hands.

RUTHVEN: True, I beg your pardon.

GRIPPER: You're extremely ungrateful! I didn't come upon you till you
    had shunted the train and done all the mischief.

RUTHVEN: True. You were just too late. If you had been one moment
    sooner—

GRIPPER: Your base design would have been frustrated! Alice would
    have gone on to Liverpool! She would have sailed to Australia with
    Herbert and married him on the voyage, and where would you
    have been?

RUTHVEN: My benefactor!

ALICE: My preserver!

ROCKALDA: My best friend!

HERBERT: My truest ally!

RUTHVEN: Gripper, tell me one thing. I've some reason to fear that my
    darling Alice, whom I worship so tenderly, and who loves me so
    fondly, turns out to be—ha! ha! my grand-daughter!

GRIPPER: No, I fancy not; I can't be sure; but if you ask *my* opinion, I
    fancy not.

RUTHVEN: My daughter deserted her little girl twenty years ago, and she hasn't turned up yet.

GRIPPER: I have thought over the matter very carefully, and putting that and that together, I have some reason to believe that I am she!

ALL: You?

GRIPPER: Yes, extravagant, isn't it? See, here is the Ms., read my description. (*Reads*) "Gripper, the most celebrated detective in the Metropolitan force, was at the same time the youngest member of it. Although of commanding stature, his face was extremely fair and his features most delicately chiselled; his hands were as soft as down, his figure was slight, indeed, almost girlish, and his voice had a touching accent in it that was invaluable to him in his assumption of female characters." That looks like it, doesn't it?

RUTHVEN: It does! My long-lost grand-daughter! (*Embraces him*)

GRIPPER: Of course, I can't be sure, but we will hope that I am mistaken.

ROCKALDA: Well, time is up! The hour is about to strike! Next time we meet we shall probably know our destinies.

No. 14: Finale to Volume 2—Ensemble.

We must depart, our masters call us,
Alas, 'tis useless to rebel;
Oh! who shall say what may befall us,
Our destiny what tongue can tell?

With my/his adored shall I/will he be mated,
Or shall I/will he wed my/his direst foe;
Oh, how we all may be related,
Upon my word, I do not know!

END OF VOLUME 2

Volume 3

<u>No. 15a: Introduction.</u>

(*Enter* HERBERT *in wedding attire*)

<u>No. 15b: RECIT. AND SONG—HERBERT.</u>

Oh, agony! and oh, despair!
My misery I cannot bear!
The novel's all but ended now,
All hope has fled!
The girl I hated—you know how—
I'm doomed to wed!
But when with me the Author's done,
And Alice Grey and I are one,
I rather think my wife
Will have good reason to regret
The luckless day when first we met!
I'll lead her such a life!

I'll sulk, and I'll fidget, and worry, and frown,
The housekeeping money I'll daily cut down;
And very poor dinners I'll make her purvey,
And someone shall dine with us every day;
I'll annoy her by superintending her rig,
Her boots shall be several sizes too big;
Her bed shall be apple-pie, sprinkled with crumbs;
Her gloves shall be cheap ones, and split at the thumbs!

Her silks shall be such as a tally-man hawks,
And I'll never allow her to bend as she walks;
High heels to her boots I shall not let her wear,
And nothing whatever shall stuff out her hair;
In second-hand bonnets my Alice shall show,
That went out of fashion a season ago;
She shall drink out of pewter, and eat out of delf,
And as for her dresses—I'll make 'em myself!

(*After song, enter* ALICE *hurriedly, in wedding dress*)

ALICE: It's infamous!

HERBERT: It's disgraceful!

ALICE: Here we are at the last chapter, and I'm just going to be married to the man I abominate!

HERBERT: And I to the woman I detest!

ALICE: And to bring me out here to Barbary, an outlandish place, with an insufficiently-clad population, and after *you*! After a milksop, who can't say boo to a goose! Oh, my friend! I'll give you such a time of it when we are comfortably married!

HERBERT: Now don't be unreasonable, Miss Grey. We are desperately in love with each other. Why should we quarrel? The remedy is within reach, I'll treat you abominably and we will be divorced.

ALICE: You promise sincerely (*shaking his hand*) You're a good-natured man after all. Forget what I said just now. Let us make the best of a bad job. How did you get from Central Africa to Algiers?

HERBERT: I walked across the desert. Didn't you read the chapter which describes my journey on foot and alone, bareheaded and barefooted from the Mountains of the Moon across the Desert of Sahara!

ALICE: No!

HERBERT: Oh it was powerfully told. For eight and forty weeks I wandered over those scorching plains supporting life on nothing particularly worth mentioning. One evening as the sun was setting in golden splendour I lay me down to die in the desert; suddenly I remembered a strange legend that the unprovided traveller need never starve in the desert of Sahara. I endeavoured to recall the rest of the legend which gave the reason why, but in vain, but seeing a caravan of Arabs in the distance I staggered towards them, and addressing their Sheik I implored him to tell me why an unprovided traveller need never starve in the desert of Sahara. "Tell me," I said, "the secret of life and the orphan's blessing shall be yours."

ALICE: And he said?

HERBERT: "That it couldn't be done for the money. The secret of life is Allah's and must be bought with a price." I tried the other Arabs one by one, but they said, "It must be bought with a price." At length I came to a swarthy Ethiopian, whose high shirt-collars and correct evening dress indicated that he was, at least, partly civilised; he wore a large frill to his shirt, and in his hands were the rib-bones of some slaughtered animal, which he rattled briskly together, as he danced wildly in the rear of the procession. I addressed him in his native language. "Thanks," said I (*imitating nigger*), "Can you tell dis child why a hunprovided traveller need never starve on the desert of Sahara? Can you told me dat?" "Iss, massa," said he, "I know dat. Yah! Yah!" "Tell me," said I, "the secret of life, and an orphan's blessing shall be yours." "Dat very old conundrum," said he, "a man need never starve on the desert of Sahara because of the *sand which is* there. Yah! Yah! Yah!" I fell fainting on the ground, for I had staked my existence on a riddle.

ALICE: And a very old one!

HERBERT: And you! How came you to Algiers?

ALICE: After I had been recognised by my father, the Duke of Ben-Nevis, I was removed into a sphere of life in which it was considered impossible for me to marry a Sunday School teacher. For a time I was happy, and thought it possible I might be intended for the infamous Sir Ruthven after all—but no, that irritating Author would not hear of it, and sent me here after you, and out I came to Algiers as—what do you think?—a female missionary to teach the dirty little black boys to read and write.

HERBERT: And what has become of the ex-Lady Rockalda?

No. 16: Melodrame.

(*Enter* ROCKALDA, *meanly dressed*)

ROCKALDA: (*Meekly*) I am here!

HERBERT: My Rockalda! and how changed! And why have you been brought out here?

ROCKALDA: I expect I am to turn up at your wedding. I rather think that stricken with remorse, I worked my passage out here as a stewardess that I might stagger into the church as you are being united, and tell you that you are no other than Sir Ruthven Glenaloon, and that he who has hitherto passed as that baronet is only poor Tom Sittybank, the bus-conductor.

HERBERT: Then I am a baronet!

ROCKALDA: You are! but you won't know it till the end of the chapter.

HERBERT: And the Sir Ruthven to whom Alice is devoted is only a mere omnibus conductor. What do you say to that, Miss Grey?

ALICE: Say! Why let me tell you a truer and a prouder heart may beat beneath the Somerset House badge of the poor omnibus conductor than beneath the lordly forehead of the haughtiest baronet. Baronet or busman, I love him, and when we are divorced he shall be mine. Where is he?

ROCKALDA: I don't know. Hasn't he come yet?

ALICE: No! It was understood that we were all to meet here just before the last chapter, and here (*turning to* Ms.) is the heading of the last chapter, and that's all.

HERBERT: I hope nothing has happened to him.

ALICE: Happened to him! Don't say that he is dead!

ROCKALDA: Dead! I most sincerely hope not. Are you in the chapter that has just been written?

ALICE: No!

ROCKALDA: Nor you?

HERBERT: No!

ROCKALDA: Nor I! Let's see what it was about. (*Takes* Ms.) It's all about Sir Ruthven (*reads*) Ha! My poor girl (*to* ALICE) I don't like you at all, but I can't help feeling for you; accept my condolences and prepare for the worst.

ALICE: The worst! Oh, read on!

ROCKALDA: Listen! (*Reads*) "Now, said Sir Ruthven, when he had ascertained by passing his thumb over the edge of the hatchet that it was sufficiently sharp for the work before it.—Now, said he, to end a life that has long been too burdensome to bear."

ALICE: (*Terrified*) Ha!

ROCKALDA: (*Reads*) "He locked the door, and going up to a cheval glass, took one long look at the magnificent but diabolical face, which had worked so much mischief in its time. As he looked he saw one solitary tear trickle from his left eye and course its way down his detestable cheek. It is the first, said he, and it shall be the last. And so saying he swung the ponderous axe three times round his head and towards the middle of the third swing the blade shot like lightning through the thickest part of the bad man's neck. The head bounded into the air and fell heavily on the floor. The lips still moved spasmodically. With a frightful effort, they managed to hiss out the dreadful words 'a very neat blow' when the jaw fell, and the vital spark departed never to return."

HERBERT: Poor Ruthven, he was a good fellow *out* of the novel.

ALICE: Now, look here, I propose we don't stand this—I propose we rebel. Let's summon the Author and have it out with him. Let's insist that the novel shall end as *we* like.

HERBERT: We will!

ALL: Author! Author!! Author!!!

(AUTHOR *enters and they attack him vociferously*)

AUTHOR: Now, ladies and gentlemen, what is it?

ALICE: You have killed Sir Ruthven!

ROCKALDA: You have murdered a true gentleman, and we insist on his being restored to life. If you don't we will never work for you again. We are conventional types; you can't get on without us.

AUTHOR: But reflect! He was such an awful scoundrel.

ROCKALDA: What he was, you made him.

AUTHOR: Well—but—(*to* HERBERT) You don't want him back, do you?

HERBERT: Most certainly!

AUTHOR: What! your hated rival, the inveterate persecutor of your beloved Alice.

HERBERT: I entirely object to his being slaughtered on my account.

AUTHOR: Magnanimous Herbert! Oh! you're a beautiful character,

ROCKALDA: Once for all, he must be restored to life.

AUTHOR: Rockalda! Consistent to the very last. She misses the abettor of all her schemes, and is helpless without him. I can quite understand it, but it can't be done.

ALICE: Oh, please give me back my love!

AUTHOR: Your love! What are you talking about? Why, he's your persecutor.

ALICE: True, but you can't think how I love him.

AUTHOR: Alice Grey! What does this mean? You are a quiet, virtuous, amiable young heroine, deeply in love with Herbert, who is a beautiful character.

ALICE: In love with Herbert! Pooh! Sir, I despise him!

AUTHOR: Oh, ridiculous!

ALICE: The man *I* love is a totally different character.

AUTHOR: But he's amiable, constant, philanthropic, mild, kind, good-tempered and (*whispers*) I'll tell you a secret—he comes into a baronetcy in the last chapter.

ALICE: I don't care; I hate mild and amiable men! I like a handsome rover, a scapegrace, a moral brigand, who sets all law at defiance. Do you suppose I'm going to marry that person? I insist on marrying Sir Ruthven, and, as a first step, he must be restored to life.

AUTHOR: But I've chopped his head off; I can't stick it on again.

ALICE: Science can do anything. Invent a process if you have it not, and if any of the critics doubt its operation, offer to prove its efficacy upon any one of them.

AUTHOR: Very good. Is there anything else?

HERBERT: Yes! I must marry Rockalda.

AUTHOR: What! the yellow-haired fiend with the panther-like movement?

HERBERT: Certainly!

AUTHOR: But you're a Sunday School teacher!

HERBERT: I don't care!

AUTHOR: I don't see how it is to be done. Will you reform her?

HERBERT: I'll try.

AUTHOR: Very good! I suppose I must give in—I don't know what my readers will say.

No. 17: Melodrame.

(*Enter* GRIPPER *dressed as a beadle*)

GRIPPER: One moment, if you please! I wish to speak to you about my fate—

AUTHOR: Oh, you're too late! We've settled everything.

ROCKALDA: Don't interfere, Gripper! You're too late. If you had been here in time you might have been consulted.

GRIPPER: But I'm bound to be late, I can't be in time. Hang it, Sir—

AUTHOR: Don't use such awful language. You don't know who you are. If you did you would be more guarded in your expressions.

GRIPPER: Then I do turn out to be somebody else?

AUTHOR: I should think you did. There's such a surprise in store for you. Listen! You are here in Algiers disguised as a protestant beadle to arrest the wicked Rockalda immediately after she has informed Herbert in the Church that he is no other than Sir Ruthven. Well, to the surprise and consternation of the clergyman and the intense delight of yourself, you turn out to be no other than—

GRIPPER: Sir Ruthven's abandoned granddaughter!

AUTHOR: (*Surprised*) Yes! How did you know that?

GRIPPER: I guessed it.

AUTHOR: That was rather sharp for a detective. Yes, you are the granddaughter. Now ain't you sorry you said, "Hang it"?

GRIPPER: No, sir, I am not, I protest against such a discovery; it's ridiculously absurd. I've been a man all my life and I protest against being changed into a woman at my time of life.

AUTHOR: But you'll be a very fine woman!

GRIPPER: I'd rather be a very fine man.

AUTHOR: You shall marry an earl.

GRIPPER: I prefer a countess!

AUTHOR: Will you let me leave it doubtful?

GRIPPER: On no account. If I am not allowed I'll never work for you again. I'm a sensation detective and you can't get on without me.

AUTHOR: Very well; I give in. You shall continue to be a man, a very fine man. That's settled. I'll alter the last chapter. Herbert shall marry Rockalda; Ruthven shall be restored to life and marry Alice; and Gripper shall turn out to be Sherlock Holmes in disguise. (*Going off*) There! What do you say to that? (*Exit*)

No. 18: FINALE TO VOLUME 3—LADY ROCKALDA, ALICE, HERBERT, GRIPPER.

ALL: I'm delighted; I'm delighted;
    All will have a happy ending.
    They will/We shall shortly be united,
    Their/Our lives together spending.

HERBERT: My Rockalda!

ROCKALDA: Oh, my Herbert!

HERBERT: I'll reform your taste for malice,

ALICE: And Sir Ruthven, dear Sir Ruthven,
    Shall be married to his Alice.

ALICE & HERBERT: To our task together warming,
    In a manner most decided,
    We will set about reforming
    Both our lovers so misguided.

ALL: To their/our task together warming,
    In a manner most decided,
    They/we will set about reforming
    Both their/our lovers so misguided.

(*Enter* SIR RUTHVEN *as a bus conductor*)

RUTHVEN: (*Rataplan*) City—Bank—City—Bank (*etc*)
ALL: I'm delighted; I'm delighted;
    All will have a happy ending.
    They will/We shall shortly be united,
    Their/Our lives together spending.

END OF VOLUME 3

CURTAIN

A Note About the Author

W.S. Gilbert (1836–1911) was an English librettist, dramatist, and poet. Born in London, Gilbert was raised by William, a surgeon and novelist, and Anne Mary, an apothecary's daughter. As a child he lived with his parents in Italy and France before finally returning to London in 1847. Gilbert graduated from Kind's College London in 1856 before joining the Civil Service and briefly working as a barrister. In 1861, he began publishing poems, stories, and theatre reviews in *Fun*, *The Cornhill Magazine*, and *Temple Bar*. His first play was *Uncle Baby*, which ran to moderate acclaim for seven weeks in 1863. He soon became one of London's most popular writers of opera burlesques, but turned away from the form in 1869 to focus on prose comedies. In 1871, he began working with composer Arthur Sullivan, whose music provided the perfect melody to some of the most popular comic operas of all time, including *H. M. S. Pinafore* (1878), *The Pirates of Penzance* (1879), and *The Mikado* (1885). At London's Savoy Theatre and around the world, The D'oyly Carte Opera Company would perform Gilbert and Sullivan's works for the next century. Gilbert, the author of more than 75 plays and countless more poems, stories, and articles, influenced such writers as Oscar Wilde and George Bernard Shaw, as well as laid the foundation for the success of American musical theatre on Broadway and beyond.

A Note from the Publisher

Spanning many genres, from non-fiction essays to literature classics to children's books and lyric poetry, Mint Edition books showcase the master works of our time in a modern new package. The text is freshly typeset, is clean and easy to read, and features a new note about the author in each volume. Many books also include exclusive new introductory material. Every book boasts a striking new cover, which makes it as appropriate for collecting as it is for gift giving. Mint Edition books are only printed when a reader orders them, so natural resources are not wasted. We're proud that our books are never manufactured in excess and exist only in the exact quantity they need to be read and enjoyed.

bookfinity™

Discover more of your favorite classics with Bookfinity™.

- Track your reading with custom book lists.
- Get great book recommendations for your personalized Reader Type.
- Add reviews for your favorite books.
- AND MUCH MORE!

Visit **bookfinity.com** and take the fun Reader Type quiz to get started.

Enjoy our classic and modern companion pairings!

Classic & Modern